TOOTHPASTE

FOR DINNER

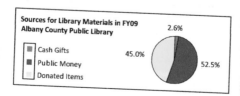

Sources for Library Materials in FY09
Albany County Public Library

- Cash Gifts
- Public Money
- Donated Items

2.6%

45.0%

52.5%

TOOTHPASTE
FOR DINNER

HOW BOOKS
F+W PUBLICATIONS, INC.
CINCINNATI, OHIO

Toothpaste for Dinner. Copyright © 2005 by Drew. Manufactured in CANADA. All rights reserved. No other part of this book may be reproduced in any form or by any electronic or mechanical means including information storage and retrieval systems without permission in writing from the publisher, except by a reviewer, who may quote brief passages in a review. Published by HOW Books, an imprint of F+W Publications, Inc., 4700 East Galbraith Road, Cincinnati, Ohio 45236. (800) 289-0963. First edition.

09 08 07 06 05   5 4 3 2 1

Distributed in Canada by Fraser Direct
100 Armstrong Avenue
Georgetown, ON, Canada L7G 5S4
Tel: (905) 877-4411

Distributed in the U.K. and Europe by David & Charles
Brunel House, Newton Abbot, Devon, TQ12 4PU, England
Tel: (+44) 1626 323200, Fax: (+44) 1626 323319
E-mail: mail@davidandcharles.co.uk

Distributed in Australia by Capricorn Link
P.O. Box 704, Windsor, NSW 2756 Australia
Tel: (02) 4577-3555

Library of Congress Cataloging-in-Publication Data

Drew.
Toothpaste for dinner : hipsters, hamsters, and other pressing issues / by Drew.
p. cm.
Includes index.
ISBN 1-58180-786-4 (pbk. : alk. paper)
1. American wit and humor, Pictorial. I. Title.
NC1429.D733A4 2005
741.5'973–dc22

2005014512

Editors: Megan Patrick, Amy Schell
Designer: Karla Baker
Production Coordinator: Kristen Heller

drew

Drew lives with his wife in Columbus, Ohio. He is the back-page columnist for the British magazine *.net* and posts a new drawing every day at www.toothpastefordinner.com. In his spare time, he records music, operates the tiny indie-rock record label Sharing Machine, and paints. He holds a patent in organic chemistry, but that and four bucks will buy you a fancy cup of flavored milky coffee.

TEFLON BACON TEST

{ TABLE OF CONTENTS }

7

PREAMBLE

Welcome to my book, whose hidden sub-sub-title is "Drawings I made while I was supposed to be working." Yes, it's true, I was supposed to be putting together spreadsheets, or typing some sort of report, or stirring chemicals together in a little dish, but I was drawing pictures instead.

I started drawing cartoons a terribly long time ago, and it wasn't out of anything other than compulsion. I compulsively draw pictures and write down ideas which please my skewed sense of aesthetics. I could never stop making weird crap, even when it was de-impressing friends and strangers when I'd make them read things I'd written or look at things I'd drawn or painted. I spent most of my time in college recording music and painting and drawing, at the expense of possibly more interesting things.

But my liver thanks my creative compulsion, and if you enjoy this book, maybe you should too, because if I hadn't practiced drawing lopsided-head people for years, they would have looked even worse today. I'll be the

first to admit that I am not "traditionally artistic." That is the nicest way I can think of to say that I could not sit down with charcoal or pastels and make a nice-looking landscape. It would end up being some scratchy drawing of some dudes standing around complaining about stuff.

My first joke was, reportedly, "The fox ate the mustard magazine." I was about three or four at the time, and after saying this to anyone, I would giggle maniacally and fall down from laughing so hard. If you flip through this book, you will see that my sense of humor has essentially not changed since. If you liked that fox joke though—boy, you are gonna totally be into the next two hundred pages. They will cut you up and put you in a box labeled "laughed so hard."

So I went to school with the dream of becoming a research chemist. I did go to school, and I did finish, and I did end up working in research. Ideally, being a research chemist is a great job. You get to think of a billion awesome ideas, and you invent inventions, and

you change peoples' lives, right? But there you are, after five years of college, stirring chemicals in a dish and then putting the chemicals in a machine to test them. Stir up a new batch and test it. Repeat for eight hours a day. Then, occasionally, type all the numbers from the tests into a computer, make a graph, circle the best mixture of chemicals, and say, "This is the best one."

Repeat for fifty-two weeks a year, for forty years, then get cancer and die. Maybe you can move up, and be the guy who tells another guy to stir up chemicals and make him a report. Or maybe you get to move up above that, and be the guy who tells several people how to mix up chemicals.

Who knows, you could even be the guy who spends every night with a short glass of scotch—sleeves all rolled up and tie loosened—watching model trains go around and around in his basement. Feel yourself sink into that folding chair as the glass slips out of your hand from the condensation collecting on its sides, and the scotch

runs down your leg to pool in your shoe. That's the American dream, the good old brass ring, and you better damn-well appreciate it.

But, what about changing peoples' lives? Oh! I forgot! That magnificent cocktail of experimental, toxic chemicals you were stirring up for months or years? Do you know what that was? It was an air freshener. Oh, what a revolution for humankind! When a man or a woman gets into his or her car, the air will smell like cloyingly-sweet fresh laundry. Or cloyingly-sweet apples. Or

throw-up-a-little-in-the-back-of-your-throat-ingly-sweet generic berry scent. Congratulations on your discovery, and the world thanks you for making its cars smell like an old lady has doused herself with half a bottle of cheap perfume and laid down in the back seat to die.

So here I am, hiding in the back of the lab to escape my eventual cancerous fate, and there you are, reading this book, and I think you will like these cartoons, so I'm tempted to say it's worked out for the best.

CHAPTER ONE
{ MOUSE TRAPS AND PING PONG BALLS }

when janitors die, they go to heaven and throw their trash on the floor, and dead CEOs and politicians have to clean it up

just kidding... there's no such thing as heaven

DEPARTMENTAL FATTENING. n. the collective name used to refer to the constant stream of birthday cake, potlucks, retirement lunches, meeting donuts, and free pizza in a typical office

TO: all.employees@work.net
SUBS: Cake in the break room at 10:30 today!

you see, son, you can't say cusses all the time... they are only for emergencies or the internet

i don't think video games influence kids... i mean, if they did, there'd be an entire internet subculture based around them, and people would stay up late every night to play them, waking up in the afternoon and pausing only to post on the internet about video games

after graduating college, i had a variety of awful jobs, like working in a can factory, and whenever i felt bad, i kept my spirits high by remembering: well, at least i'm not in grad school

WHAT COLLEGE PROFESSORS
WANT YOU TO BELIEVE HAPPENS:

DREW!!! we are in way over our heads on this one! we're gonna lose this account unless you can do a triple integral in polar coordinates and show all work!!

do graphic designers go christmas
cropping in december

i scanned in some pictures
from your desk and cut
you out of them

this is what the world
would be like... if you
were NEVER BORN

NEVERRRRRR
BORRRRNNN

oh man, they're
playing in
cleveland, but
not in columbus

when your favorite band is on
tour, but they don't come to
your city, and the nearest stop
is two hours away, and you don't
want to drive all that way to
see them, you are old

in every office... there is one
cubicle... which will never forget

NINE ELEVEN COWORKER: WHY
DO THEY STILL HAVE ALL THOSE
POSTERS, IT'S KIND OF EMBARRASSING

when i was a kid,
i had to go out back
of the office, hand-
pump the coffee, and
carry it back in pails

if i can ever bring the rapping
bum together with the bum who
reads everything he sees out loud,
i will have created an unstoppable
musical force

help is on
the way!
buckeyes
are here
to stay!

student special
four for five
dollars, new
taste deals

thanks to the recent military
action i can finally resume
my favorite hobby from 1991:
scratching off the T and
the leg of the R on patriotic
stickers so they read:

SUPPORT OUR POOPS

HAMSTER you chewed up the pieces of wood i gave you, ate all the sunflower seeds i set out, and crapped all over the nice soft litter i put in your cage! THIS IS WHY WE CAN'T HAVE ANYTHING NICE

this is your captain speaking, i'd like to remind you all to keep your seatbelts on during the entire flight, on account of me being totally roasted

i was just thinking about how you could use thin pieces of cardboard to support weight and be very strong

i came up with a system to fold and glue the sheets

then i realized: i just invented corrugated cardboard

great job dude

FUN FACT:
did you know that flying
squirrels can't actually fly?
instead, they use special
glands to levitate and hover,
much like a helicopter

why do the weirdest people
in the world only leave
their houses to go to malls
and rock shows

EXCERPT FROM "THE UNEMPLOYMENT DICTIONARY":

week-end. n. the two days that you have to find something else to do, because web sites do not update

afterbeef. n. the short, percussive conclusion to a long or powerful beef

froooooooeeee... POP

today i put on my belt and it was tighter than usual

upon examination, i had accidentally put a half twist in the belt and worn a MOBIUS BELT for over ten minutes

I WEAR THE MOBIUS BELT!!! I AM THE TAILOR OF THE VERY FABRIC OF THE UNIVERSE

HOW TO TELL YOU ARE OLD: PART 2

when you hurt your back jumping on the bed and you realize you are too old and fragile to ever do it again

GRANDPA IN A STARTER
JACKET
- where did he get it
- kinda weird

dude-ic acid

i was going to get divorced,
but i got left at the altar

the altar of divorce
altarrrrr of divorrrrrce

what is my hobby, it is to put
bags inside other bags

in hell, it is always
10 am, you are always
hungry, and the vending
machine won't accept
dollar bills

then, after you finish sixteen years
of school, you get to go to work!
unlike school, which is full of petty,
cruel children who have constructed
a bizarre society of conformance
through verbal and physical abuse, work
is full of petty, cruel adults who have
constructed a bizarre society of
conformance through threats of
dismissal! so cheer up, your whole life
is in front of you

i am not only the president of the beard of the month club...

i am also the vice president

THE MOST UNNECESSARY
THING EVER:

i'm in the
dorito aisle,
do you want
cool ranch or
nacho cheese,
over

CELL PHONE
WALKIE TALKIES

i have created the world's most powerful car sticker! it bears an image of calvin, peeing on an upside-down calvin, who is in turn peeing on the first calvin! if applied to a regular car, the sheer force of opinion could cause the entire known universe to implode!!

rivvit
rivvit

when i was a kid, i used
to move the zipper back
and forth on my jacket
as fast as i could, and
pretend i was a rapper

what is gossip? well, son,
gossip is like a present,
and each time you tell
someone else, you get to
open it again

you took all the papers i gave you to file, stuffed them into the sink, and left the water running

oh, sorry, i'm just a temp

no matter what you do, you can excuse your behavior by simply saying "sorry, i'm just a temp"

gettin real inopportune
like a bowl of saskatoon
but you know i'm where it's at
like MEDICINE HAT

my theoretical future rap
career includes a song
where i give short-outs to
canadian cities whose
names i like

all it takes is two
pencils taped to your
head to transform
any office into a deadly
cubicle maze, where all
who get lost meet a
grisly death at the
hands of OFFICE MINOTAUR!!

 if you're driving down a long straight road on a hot summer day and the road looks like it's wet, even if it's not, that means you have cancer

over there is the rarest of
all species: the white-collared
middle manager! now, i've gotta
be real careful, because he has
a natural defense mechanism
which shifts blame to
subordinate employees

COFFEE, 12 oz.

WARNING: excess consumption may lead to completion of assignments, heightened creativity, disappearance of headaches, and/or unbridled joy

DREW: COFFEESHOP BLACK
OPS SPECIALIST

when you get up from
your clean, non-wobbly
table, i will know. and
i will take it.

HOW TO TELL WHEN YOU ARE OLD: PART 3

babies everywhere

congratulations

when people your age tell others they are pregnant, everyone congratulates them instead of saying "...ohhh" or just sucking air in through their teeth

CHAPTER TWO

{ NO BIRTHDAY CAKE FOR THE DOG }

sometimes at work i smell something foul and walk around for a few minutes trying to find what it is coming from, before i realize it is just the stench of my fast-approaching mortality

FUN FACT:
fish can't smell

i haven't
showered
in days

it's cool,
i can't
smell

yeah, i'm pretty much living out the american dream

not only did i marry someone with health insurance, but thanks to the declining value of the dollar, i'm paying less rent every day hey, drew, you can type, right? i need you to type up these forty-seven pages of notes before tomorrow

every year, hundreds of coworkers are injured by punches to the head and face, caused by asking me to do completely retarded things for them

go on, play vith it
now, you hef fun

the worst part of my seventh
birthday was when i realized
that my grandpa was only one
of thousands who were too
cheap to buy a real slinky, and
that instead, he took an old, rigid
truck spring from his garage
and gave it to me

how was your
weekend

my family did another
stupid intervention

they were all like "drew,
we care about you...
you're not going to find
life's answers at the
bottom of a coffee cup"

BUSINESS TIP:

try inserting sound effects
into slideshow presentations
to make them more exciting
and dynamic

for best results, use this tip
on coworkers' or supervisors'
files when they are not at
their desks

HAMSTER i don't care if you live in a cage, you still do not need to trade me cigarettes for favors

i got a new job the other
day, and for a second i
was worried that i wouldn't
have anything to write
about, because it's not
too bad

then i remembered: it
takes exactly two weeks
for every single job to
turn to crap

is this
your card

no

THEN GO
TO YOUR
ROOM

i always hated magic
tricks as a child

when i was born, my baby mommy put me in a basket and set it on the doorstep of my baby daddy with a note taped to my head that said YOU ARE MY DAD and that is pretty much the reason i am breaking up with you

whoa-ho
whoa-ho-hoa
whoaaa

every thursday night
i go out to "backup
karaoke" at the
local bar

OPHTHALMOLOGIST i need you
to hold very still, you will
just feel a tiny puff of air

the last time i was in
a mall store, some lady
sprayed me with cologne

i gave her a shot of
pepper spray and asked
if she would like the
whole bottle at twenty
percent off

ALL NEW!!

a padded thing to sit on while you watch stadium sports!

warning: padded thing will not alleviate the feeling that ya're wasting your life watching steroid-laden men chasing each other around in a field, slapping other men on the butt

eat them up,
yum...... fish
heads, fish heads,
roly poly fish
heads

have you ever wondered: is
he/she "the one"? if you made
a tape as a child with only
the song "fish heads" over and
over, and upon mention of
this to your significant othe-
they admit to doing the same,
your search is over

scientific studies have
shown that yelling "where
are the damn twist ties"
actually doubles the time
an average person takes
to find the twist ties

if you smell your hands right after touching a bunch of pennies, it is easy to accidentally think that you are a robot

man, gas is
so expensive
these days

oh, man, for real! i mean,
it's almost like it is not
free to drill oil out of the
ground, ship it to the
refinery, make gasoline out
of it, and fill thousands
of trucks with the gas
and drive them all over
the country to gas stations

SCHROEDINGER'S DECAF

hey is that regular or decaf

no one knows whether it is regular or decaf! there is a fifty percent chance of each, and until we can taste it, we must assume the coffee to simultaneously be both regular and decaf

fashion is a competition between
people to see who can look the
most like a retarded clown

well, son, all i know is that
when we die, we never have
to listen to smooth jazz ever
again, so if you ever get
worried, just think of that

ACTUAL CONVERSATION
I HEARD IN THE GAS
STATION THE OTHER DAY

mom can i get
a candy bar

okay... but if i
get you a candy
bar, that'll be
your only snack
for after dinner
today

drew's rule of
grandparents:

the meanest
ones always
live the longest

lightning bugs: too slow
to resist catching, but
too bitter to eat more
than a handful at one
sitting

my current research deals with finding a television show that has a laugh track as well as actual humor

so far i have failed

FUN FACT:
all IT employees are
required to grow and
maintain this beard,
as mandated by federal
law

when i'm having a rough week
at work, i like to come in
early on friday, take the cables
from every computer in my
department, and put them in
a box in the hallway labeled
"FREE"

 i would like to propose a
compromise with respect
to marijuana use, so that
we can finally solve this
issue

my plan is that marijuana
will be legalized, but jam
bands, patchouli, and hemp
products will be outlawed

i found this in your room... a passport, son? did you really think you could travel to other countries without your mother and i knowing?

yep, here it is, just like i told you - the government says they're going to take away your legos unless you go clean them up right now

i'm sorry, son, my hands are tied, i guess you gotta clean up your room

if you have a second-story window but no megaphone, you are missing out on one of life's greatest pleasures

why don't you unbalance
this, you son of a
washtub

want to work from home?
create your own work schedule?
then we have something for
you!

UNEMPLOYMENT- ten million
americans can't be wrong!

whenever i get depressed
thinking about how i
can't retire from my
job for at least thirty
more years, i think: well,
maybe i'll die before
that, and won't have to
work that long after all

number of times
an average person
will lean too hard
on a towel bar: 1

my score to date: 4

what happens to a
dream deferred? does
it stink up the
building like a fish
locked in your desk
on your last day
of work?

why didn't bach
go to the movies!
because he
was baroq—

because he died
prior to their
creation

drew you have been late twice this week. i printed off part of the employee code for you to read and remind yourself about the rules here

oh, hey, thanks! i just printed off this page explaining how i won't start to care until i get paid a living wage

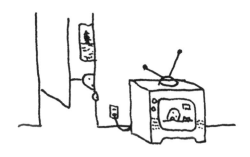

when i was little, i could hear
a high-pitched sound whenever a
television was on anywhere -
even if the volume was turned
all the way down and i was
in the next room

nobody else i knew could hear it
so i thought i had something
wrong with me

CHAPTER THREE

{ BATTERIES ARE DELICIOUS }

Welcome to ThirdParty Office!

I see that you started a new document. Do you need help in:

- Screed explaining why Democrats and Republicans are the same
- Screed demanding equal media coverage
- Screed comparing Canadian elections to US elections
- General screed template

i don't care how many
grad students tell you
otherwise, sweat is not
"the body's natural shower"

why did the man watch japanese animation movies

because he was overweight and did not have friends

i dunno

QUICK TIP: are you a parent? if so, remember who will choose your nursing home

SHADY SHITTERS
FECAL HOME
FOR
THE SHITTY

ATTENTION ALL ZOOS:

you could make millions off me alone if you had a dog section in the zoo

clearly i am not the only one who would pay the entrance fee if it meant i were guaranteed to see at least one boston terrier

and now, let's dim the lights,
so i can show you computer
slides, and read the exact
text of the slides to you

the scientist's dilemma:

buy an air conditioner, or just change the laws of physics to make his house cooler?

that was excellent! okay,
now it's your turn to stand
here for twenty minutes
while i talk to you about
my own medical problems

a few months ago, i learned that one of my ancestors once killed another man with a shovel

that either means i have strong genes, or that i have inherited the tendency to drink too much

do you ever have this
dream? if so, watch out
for my eyeballs, i don't
know where they are

crap, i should have
charged my π-pod
before i left

so i see you have
a bachelor's degree...
what did you
major in

i majored in bidness

nunyo bidness

PANFLUTE FLOWCHART

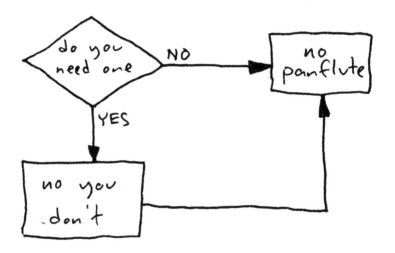

we have worked for decades
to create a product with
the highest pork density
on earth, and finally we
have succeeded

now available for the
first time ever: the hotdog-
flavored pork rind

happy birthday! now blow
out all the candles on
your birthday steak

drew, i will be
out of the office
this afternoon,
see you tomorrow

translation: drew, go home
at one o'clock

TEENAGERS:

yet another reason to never have children

from now on, all emails
must be written in
iambic pentameter

what to do with
an english degree

i have arranged this
month's expense
report into short
sections of seventeen
spreadsheet cells, in
the pattern 5-7-5

i feel it reflects the beauty and
balance present in the forms and
shapes of our department

SCIENCE TRIVIA:

did you know that the more members an instrumental rock band has, the worse they are? studies have shown the optimum number is zero

i hate you
forever dad

the one bad thing
about naming your
son "banjo"

... in fact, four out
of five doctors
agree: SHUT UP

hey man, congrats on that early retirement

uh... nothin

what

sometimes, as i pass middle managers in the hall, i tell them, "congratulations on your early retirement!" and when they are surprised, act like i wasn't supposed to tell them

uh huh
uh huh
yeah
uh huh
yeah
yeah
uh huh

I BET YOU HAVE
TO WORK WITH
THIS GUY TOO

as your father, i have to tell you — don't take drugs unless you think staying up all night writing poetry using only the word "dog" is a major life achievement

the last time i went
fishing, it was THIS DUMB

no, wait, more like this

then my finger was extending, like - reeeooowwwww, and it dipped into the whipped cream ten feet away and put it in my mouth

the only thing worse than going to work is going to work and listening to coworker drug stories

son, after last weekend, i thought
i should get you this book... it
has some things we've already
talked about in it, but i think
you will enjoy it anyway

it is called "chicken soup for
we all wish grandma would hurry
up and die, but you can't say it
out loud"

we're going to need
you to re-code the
entire database
by hand

that's
retarculous*

*retarded plus ridiculous. canadian
translation: "saskatchewhoa"

every time a cell phone
rings, an angel gets
kinda annoyed

here is one for free... if you like it, you know where to get more

as a child i bought bulk candy at the supermarket and resold it to my classmates at tremendously inflated prices

my empire was huge but it crumbled quickly when i started trying my own merchandise

THE SCRABBLE CLUB

the other day while i
was at the coffee shop
i happened upon the
scrabble club

their apparent leader
was a cold man who
shook the bag of tiles
violently as he stared
at his opponent - even
the nine-year-old who
appeared to be his
son

i have invented the best condiment ever: POP TART SAUCE!!

now, you can have the doughy, overly-sweet taste of pop tarts on your favorite foods... or just eat it straight from the bottle!!

hey sheila... uh, i'm gonna
be going to oregon this
weekend. so do you know
if there's any way i
could just get paid in
oxen? i'll need a few,
some of em are gonna
drown when we ford
rivers

as words become increasingly popular and trickle down through social classes to reach children, they inevitably change to represent one half of the binary good/bad classification:

1981: awesome
1985: gay
1989: bad (i.e., good)
1992: sweet
2003: islamic
2006: downsized
2011: apocalyptic

aw man, my charles dickens rap action figure broke... totally downsized

whenever my coworkers tell me any kind of story, i like to dismiss it with "oh, that's just an urban legend!"

if i had a dollar for
every time i had sixty
cents, i would be canada

i think i need to find
a roommate

my refrigerator is so full
of food it's about to break,
and my sink and trash
can are perpetually
clean and empty

hey, i couldn't make
the meeting this
afternoon, so i called
the secretary and
rescheduled it for
never

you have
acromegaly

a glandular
disorder
characterized
by swelling
of the hands
and feet

what

no i
don't

as a child, i would often use
rare medical insults to
confuse my peers and lead
them into the "if your hand
is bigger than your face, you
have cancer" trap

CHAPTER FOUR

{ DO YOU COME HERE OFTEN }

life is pretty much like ikea furniture; no matter how many times you read the instructions, it quickly comes to a short, brutal end

TOOTHPASTE FOR DINNER

BUTCHER do you call this
a london broil, it is
barely even a top round

SORRY WON'T CUT A
LONDON BROIL MISTER

sorry
drew

presenting the TOASTJET 5000.!! prints on any kind of toast, and comes with easily-refillable jam and peanut butter cartridges!

WELCOME TO THE FUTURE

i will insist on going
to the expensive buffet
and then only eat ham
cubes for dinner!

yet another reason to
never have children

HAMSTER i am tired of giving you handouts, you are going to have to earn your keep from now on

so before i give you this wood thing to chew on, i want to hear a short freestyle rap on the subject of hamster gang affiliations

last night i woke up and
wrote down an idea from a
dream i had which i knew
would help the country

i read it when i woke up
this morning and it said:

800 NIPPLE-HANDS ARE
NEEDED TO START THE
REVOLUTION

CARGO SHORTS VS. CAPRI PANTS

the final match in the 2006 world cup of clothes that make you look dumb

cats: somewhere, one
is thinking right now
about how much it
hates you

cheer up, kiddo

when you get older
you'll be able to drink
until you're so chronically
debilitated you can't form
new memories at all

i've thought about it
for a while, and if i
ever start rapping, my
rap name will be
DI$COUNT$

then, if i do a solo
project later, it'll be
called $AVING$

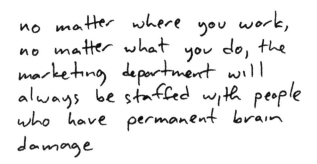

double-sided tape is OUT!
we need something fresh...
tape that is sticky on
THREE SIDES!!

no matter where you work,
no matter what you do, the
marketing department will
always be staffed with people
who have permanent brain
damage

your personal ad
said you were
"athletic" and
weighed a hundred
fifty pounds!!

arrr, tis a
hundred fifty
nautical pounds

my favorite
"the finger"
method:

cranking the
drawbridge

if you do not think humans
evolved from monkeys, all
you have to do to change
your opinion is to see the
boogers people put on the
wall in almost every bathroom
in every place i have ever
worked

okay, now move your arms up, and down, and up, and down, and up, and now reach, reach, reach, good, now give me a dollar

introducing the revolutionary new exercise system: HOBOFLEX

WARNING:

constantly printing out things all day long may lead to a higher incidence of head punches caused by coworkers

there are 10 types
of people in the
world: people who
understand binary,
and people who
have friends

hey copier, have you seen space jam, the movie about a cartoon and a basketball player? yeah, well they're making a sequel called paper jam, and it stars you, and my foot kicking you

i would rather rearrange
letters that begin words
than confront my
alcoholism

the last time i was at the post office, some dude with long hair and black jeans was taking forever to pick what kind of stamps he wanted, so i told him, HURRY IT UP DUNGEONMASTER!!

he got kinda mad, so in retrospect maybe i should have said, GET A MOVE ON COMMANDER KEEN

you can pick your friends,
and you can poop at work,
but you can't chase your
work friends around with
a piece of poop

hey there, partner... are you
shirkin' hard, or hardly shirkin'?

 make up to two thousand dollars a month stuffing envelopes! use receipts, paper clips, other peoples' hair, things you find on the sidewalk! FILL YOUR CLOSETS WITH BROKEN APPLIANCES!! EAT NOTHING BUT APRICOTS!!!! THE WORLD IS YOURS

CORPORATE POLICY CHANGE:
all employees are now required
to carry a hoop at all times,
and to jump through it prior
to the completion of any task.
failure to do so will be grounds
for dismissal.

are you wondering where
you fit into the world?

do you ever wonder what
it all means?

is your blood sugar unstable
due to your body's inability
to produce insulin?

the answers to these, and other
important questions, lie in one
book... DIABETICS

scientists have discovered that the number of nights per week you cry yourself to sleep is directly proportional to how much you like the lord of the rings

i used to make coffee with a french press - a cylinder with a mesh strainer that brews coffee grounds when you pour in hot water

i switched over last week to an american press... it works the same, but it ignores my failures and tells the entire world that i'm doing a great job brewing coffee

hey drew,
whatcha doin'

just about to
get on a
conference call
here in a
minute

translation: going to hide
in the bathroom and do
mad libs by myself for
an hour

bobby, you may be wondering why i invited you over here today... we're going to do a little experiment called "do you have five dollars, because mr. wizard's pension is barely enough to cover his cable bill"

there comes a time in everyone's life
when they must ask themselves:
am i SERIOUS about being unemployed?

not serious | not serious | not serious | not serious | serious

my fellow americans, our world-wide oil reserves are at an all-time low, which is a strong and immediate threat to the american way of life

that is why, earlier today, i signed a bill from congress declaring war on dinosaurs, who are directly responsible for this global threat to our oil supply

we will stop these terrorists, and turn them into fossil fuel at any cost

and then, when you love someone enough to live with them for six to eighteen months, you can get starter married too

what's fo-
lunch
today

soul-crushing melancholy
followed by a long
complacent torpor until
i find relief in death

oh, sorry, i thought you
said "what's the rest
of your life going to
be like"

if you're not part
of the solution,
you're part of the
precipitate

i'm sorry, we don't have any open positions right now

that can mean only one thing: SOMEONE MUST DIE

people who take
more ketchup packets
than they are going
to use...
CAUGHT ON TAPE

what's up, yahoo games
click here to find your
match on yahoo personals

once i walked into a coworker's
office as he was playing online
backgammon, and until he quit his
job, every time i saw him i would
call him "yahoo games"

and then, i pulled thru and picked up my order and it was WRONG!

it's almost like the place is run by a multi-national corporation who beefs up its profits by underpaying its apathetic seventeen-year-old employees

to hunt the wild hipster,
one must replicate its
mating call exactly

the best way to end a
conference call is by shouting
"fifteen percent, take it or leave
it!!", regardless of what you
are discussing

CHAPTER FIVE

{ KINDA WEIRD (WHERE DID HE GET IT) }

life is like a grocery conveyor belt... we emerge and shortly disappear into the checkout aisle thing and in between, we have eggs and milk put on top of us, and...

uh, the one thing stops it when stuff passes by

TOOTHPASTE FOR DINNER

and that is the difference
between alternating curry
and direct curry

THIS DAY IN CHEMISTRY HISTORY:

1952: sensing a lack of hilarity in the field, the english chemist p. walter henries renames the little rubber scraper that attaches to a stirring rod a "rubber policeman".

in a world...
where nothing
is what it
seems

when work gets slow, i like to
put my glasses on upside
down and walk around talking
like i am in a movie trailer

after an exhaustive study we have concluded that the only way to improve the classic flip-flop is to rename it to something more evocative of its grandeur

ladies and gentlemen, i present to you... THE FLAP-FLAP!!

CHAIN MEMOS

here's a memo for you... now, remember,
you have to copy it and post it on
seven bulletin boards within the next
week, or you will be in trouble

one man in the chicago branch
forgot to make copies before posting,
and the next day, his coffee mug
was gone

last year, i went to
california, to visit a
city called "los
angeles"

in english, that means
"the angeles"

ugh, the bathroom
smells terrible

yeah, it's almost
as if people go
in there and
just pull down
their pants and
poop

son, the reasons you can't get a dog go beyond the fact that your mother will end up feeding him... it's... well... i'll put it this way: if i pay for a dog, i'm naming him, and it will embarrass you to tell your friends that your dog is named "hobo snot"

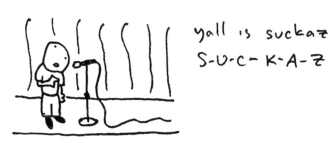

yall is suckaz
S-U-C-K-A-Z

in the seventh grade i made it to the regional spelling bee, but did not advance due to receiving too many technical fouls

beedle
deedle
donk

thanks to technology, the most annoying sound in the world is no longer people listening to bleepy ring-tones in public, but instead, people listening to all their phone's available midi songs

martin, i was looking
for some files, and i
found this in your desk...
you know as well as i
do that the rules of
the company state that
marshmallow fluff
must only be eaten on
sandwiches, and not
straight from the jar

while the cucumber burp
is widely regarded as
the worst flavor of
burp in the scientific
community, there is
little but anecdotal
evidence to suggest
that the carrot cake
burp is indeed the best

lego man why are you
here? there is no reason
for it

PREPARE TO BE
EXISTENTIALIZED

if i ever have kids, they will
get THE EXISTENTIAL
PLAYSET for christmas
it is composed of all their other
toys, plus a shop vac, so that
occasionally, one of them will
get sucked into the void
for no reason

thank you for calling the
drew show... caller, go ahead

well, caller, this is pretty
common... i suggest you crush
his ambitions until he loses
the will to live

hey drew, i
love your show!
anyway, i
called to ask-
how do i get
my son to §stop
jumping on the
bed?

for example, if he wants to
be a fireman, tell him that
he'll never be a fireman, no
matter how hard he tries.
then drown his guinea pig.
that'll do it. next caller
go ahead

thank you
for shopping
at pirateco

if i were a pirate and
i ran a small store, i
would keep receipts on
my hand hook

portrait of the self-made
immunologist

putting pens,
pencils, doorknobs,
etc. in mouth

healthy
immune
system

gang sines

dammit, where'd i put
my keys at

i'll help you look for
them, as soon as you
put a dollar in the
"end a sentence with
a preposition" jar

NEW ADVENTURES IN OFFICE MUZAK HELL:

an all-MIDI instrumental version of "tom's diner"

toot toot toot-toot
toot toot too-toot,
toot toot too-toot
too-toot too-toot
(synth-brass)

some days, when the weather is nice, i like to put on my lab coat and stand on the side walk and tell people, "if my calculations are correct, you did not shower today!" or "if my calculations are correct, you are wearing a watch and can tell me what time it is"

DUST

dust is made of bad
thoughts and mean words,
so you need to only do
nice things from now on
because your mother is
tired of vacuuming

yaaaaahhh

toys toys toys

PARENTS: do you let your kids run around inside stores, yelling the whole time? if so, i'm sure you want to know what some snide twenty-something thinks you oughta do about it

i would recommend
the double almond
cloaca

i hate to sound racist, but
i can't stand going to the
coffee shop when that damn
komodo dragon is working

the other day i found
a bunch of easter egg
colors in the closet

so i bought six dozen
eggs, colored them, and
hid them all over the
side of my neighbor's
house and car

and now i lay thee to rest, keyboard #2 that i have destroyed in as many months

both fought bravely but could not overcome the destructive power of diet cherry soda

i'll be back in a few
minutes, i have to
drop the kids off at
the lake

okay

wait, i thought
you didn't have
kids

my greatest regret is
that i never filled
entire notebooks with
obsessive, paranoid
writing and left them
for my family to
discover

oh no

last night a bat got inside and wouldn't leave, so i hit it with a broom and then realized: oh no, what if a goth finally figured out how to turn into a bat and i killed it?!

HELPFUL TIP:
when i first start dating
someone, i go through their
trash and write down a list
of the personal hygeine
items they use

then, i send them the list,
along with a small note
that says: USE THESE

FOOD FIGHT

FOOD FIIIIIGHT!!!

every so often, i like
to grab my tray and
stand up in the
cafeteria at work, and
yell "food fight!", just
in case

why was the summer
movie a multi-million
dollar hit

because the american
public does what
commercials tell it to

i dunno,
why

you look down
partner, what-
cha thinkin
about

oh, i'm not sad,
i was just thinking
about making
drawings on an
orange, using a
magnifying glass
to focus sunlight
and burn it

when people at work ask me
what i am thinking about, i
like to tell them exactly what
i am thinking about

QUICK TIP:

speak softly and carry
someone's ripped-off arm
around with you

no matter how far
technology advances,
there will never be a
better computer
accessory than dot
matrix printer paper

you can be anything
you want to be when
you grow up if you
are rich!!

my neighborhood is great - any time i want, i can go out and find a pickup game of "yell at hipsters"

hipsterrrr!

pleated slacks:
why aren't they
illegal

children are like flowers, oh-ho
who forgot how to grow

deaf people are like flowers, hey hey
who forgot how to hear

INDEX

TOOTHPASTE FOR DINNER